Experience Redefining to Find that Silver Lining

Catriona McDonald

BookLeaf Publishing

India | USA | UK

Presentation by *BookLeaf Publishing*

Web: www.bookleafpub.com

E-mail: info@bookleafpub.com

ISBN: 9789358319989

First edition 2024

Sinister Strings Attached to Things

Be very quiet and still and you might hear a
message from a top inventor of money
the Mulberry trees

They want you to know that their paper won't
solve all your worries

It's not more money that you are craving and you
don't wish to add to your plethora of shoes

To only be wealthy by materialism will leave
you feeling empty and dejected

At least that seems to be nature's views

Seasonal Affective Disorder

When the weather was balmy and dry
a morning hike held a significant allure

Now it's always cold and wet
Unfortunately seasonal depression is common
with no proven cure

It's the little things in life
that will get you through your day

Enjoy a cup of coffee inside
while you feel the weight of the world fall away

Watch as the only ephemeral ray of sun
gleams off your window pane

And try to remember there is no rainbow
nor flowers
without a downpour of rain

Body Positivity vs Body Neutrality

When the world keeps telling you view your
body as beauteous
and to accept your ill-favoured physical flaws

Repeating the affirmation "I love my cellulite"
feels as real to you as Santa Claus

Although you are flawless in every way
focus on what functions your body can do for
you instead

Your legs give you the ability to walk, run and
dance
Moreover they got you out of bed

Your body can change
but your worth does not

Missing out due to appearance
makes for a bland and nondescript life plot

Healthier coping mechanisms

There is a monster called Void
who indissolubly lives on the frame of your bed

You manage to escape him by immersing
yourself in addictions
as you yearn for just a moment of quietude
inside of your head

You don't need to shrink him
but to face all his challenges with vigor
for he is only reality
and you are much bigger

Number 1 Motivator

5

If you can be your own worst critic
then you can be your own best friend

Motivation can come after you start
so take the first step by believing you can do it
and soon you'll start to comprehend

First and foremost you must
reward yourself with a treat
for your new attainment

You deserve to enjoy it and celebrate
even when there's no one around
to witness your achievement

The Limitless Label

The child with monocular vision
is told she should no longer read aloud to the
class

Yet she outperforms her peers in geography
Her drawings are exceptional
The test result states 100% Pass

Her mind befogged by this predicament
She realises labels can create a self-fulfilling
prophecy

Her life's been full of challenges
and quite the odyssey

Labels come with pros and cons
As a steadfast student
she promises to always try

She knows she can do anything
except learn to fly

Still she identities as
'the superhero with only one eye'

Notification: You Have 15 New Likes

If their compliments imbue you
with feelings of glee

If their criticism changes your mood
then you are not free

Both should feel netural
because you know yourself best

If you fail to relate
put a social media detox to the test

Independence is a Blessing & a Curse

The lone wolf emerges from her light slumber

It's her first winter hunting independently
She considers herself puissant and stronger

She was the confident bellwether of her old wolf
pack

They were slower and weaker
Now she eats every day
They're no longer holding her back

As darkness falls, she spots an oak tree to sleep
under
Unfortunately the risk of freezing to death
tonight remains high for her once again

The pack go to bed hungry
but the weather changes are of little concern
As all they huddle together safe and warm in
their den

A Train Journey through Time and Space

Sandwiched between two strangers on your
usual weekend commute back home, your mind
begins to wander

The drunk passenger who often gets ignored
might have lost someone recently and maybe
that's why he tends to maunder

As a group of discourteous teenagers board,
everyone looks down at their phone, to avoid
any potential strife

Your little brother dresses like they do but you'd
describe him as quite the erudite

You always keep your replies short, so perhaps
they think you're glib, you begin to ponder

You do your best to be amiable as you know that
everyone is living a life as complex and vivid as
your own

For that is the meaning of sonder

Appreciate Your Animal Companion

Take a moment of gratitude for your furry friend

As they lay supine on your lap feeling undying
love for you that'll last til the end

You meet their needs
and they meet yours too

With a lick of your hand,
they say, Thank you.

Can I Speak with The Manager Please?

If your humdrum job has you feeling ennui

Use your mellifluous voice and sing something
cheery

When work problems are perennial
think of a fond memory
remain calm and genial

Some days the public display rancor
they cannot help but sneer and jeer

One thing is unambiguously clear
You'll never cease to persevere

Modern War Dystopia

As one country becomes exonerated
it's now our turn to persecute the other

From the comfort of your home please pick
which village these fumes should now smother

When there is only one race, the human race

To support any form of nationalism can only be
described as a complete disgrace

Until we respect all people
irrespective of colour and creed

Knavish bankers will take delight in lining their
pockets as the innocent are left in the wreckage
to bleed

I Wish You Could See What I See

Secretly, they find your beauty ineffable
And your delicate voice is simply unforgettable

With a face so radiant and comely
and an attitude so optimistic and jaunty

You gleefully welcome the sunshine in
You no longer feel crestfallen as it touches your
skin

You've emerged from the darkness feeling jovial
again
You were once crowned beautiful but never in
vain

Cosy Autumn Sun

You stand under an amber ray of sun

It may be a serene setting but the day has only
just begun

You go gambolling through the forest and
marvel at the height of the deciduous trees

You've run so far you get the dulcet scent of an
ocean breeze
It's then you look up to see a grey cloudlet form

It's time to get back home where you'll be safe
and warm

Grab a soothing hot drink and listen to the
tempest storm

A Merciful God

15

Repent of all your sins
God will harken your sorrowful prayers and will
be delighted to now
put you on the right path

Even when disaster strikes
Your newfound faith will never flee
while those who mock God
will oftentimes feel his wrath

No one is superior as we are all sinners
but it would be nice to see you again
flawless and clothed in white

Holy scripture denotes
If you don't make it into heaven
I won't remember your existence
As you'll be in the dark
while I bask in his light

Dare To Dream

What is the meaning of a numinous dream?

When we remember them upon waking, is it a
lesson things are not as 3D as they seem?

Do the supernal angels you meet have a special
message for you?

Your limiting beliefs could be holding you back
from your truest virtue

Be a Silly Billy

Don't forget to laugh when you trip and fall

Tell your family silly stories sure to amuse them
all

So lithe and fit your infinite amount of energy
will have you feeling immortal

To regain your zest for life please step through
☆The Innerchild Portal☆

Let this be a jolly reminder to act a fool!
Regain some innocence
It'll make you cool

Don't go Raging about Ageing

Ageing is a gift
please show love to yourself today

You may become less telegenic but
your perky personality is here to stay

Some are pulchritudinous yet nefarious

Focusing on maintaining a pretty aesthetic will
leave you feeling precarious

Mr Squirrel's Secret Side Quest

Peering out of the kitchen window at dusk, you
spot a squirrel full of mirth up on a tree branch
where he is stacking his ample supply of nuts

To leap while holding it all will require him to
have some guts.

In the distance you see the local beldam's fat,
black cat, trudging along in the tree's direction.

You tap the window and let out a sigh of relief
because he successfully fled, all thanks to your
protection

He made a blunder that cost him to drop most of
his food

Jubilant no more, he disappears from your eyes'
view into the tree hollow to sit and brood

Using a torch you begin to pick up the chestnuts
that are now scattered all around.

Love thy neighbour even when they reside a
little lower to the ground

Dare to be You

Why wouldn't you be yourself when there is no
such thing as the perfect personality

Everyone views you from the unique perspective
of their own individuality

Once you have this epiphany you may now
adopt this quintessential trait

Authenticity is the key to being both joyful and
prosperous
Use it to unlock the gate

Truth Teller

Amass the courage to speak the truth
even though your voice may tremble

It'd be craven of you to keep it inside
so an egregious lie you should disassemble

Some will take umbrage
others will titter then stare

Your words may go unheeded
but you should not care

www.ingramcontent.com/pod-product-compliance
Lightning Source LLC
LaVergne TN
LVHW050310200726
843509LV00015B/3249